SIT
WALK
STAND

The Process *of* Christian Maturity

WATCHMAN NEE

PUBLICATIONS

Fort Washington, PA 19034

Sit, Walk, Stand, **Trade Paper Edition**

Published by CLC Publications

U.S.A.
P.O. Box 1449, Fort Washington, PA 19034

GREAT BRITAIN
51 The Dean, Alresford, Hants. SO24 9BJ

AUSTRALIA
P.O. Box 469, Kippa-Ring, QLD 4021

NEW ZEALAND
10 MacArthur Street, Feilding

ISBN 13: 978-0-87508-973-7

Scripture quotations are from the
American Standard Version, 1901.

Italics in Scripture are the emphasis of the author.

This printing 2010

Printed in the United States of America

Contents

Preface to the Fourth Edition

COMPILED from the spoken ministry of Mr. Watchman Nee (Nee To-sheng) of Foochow and first published in Bombay, *Sit, Walk, Stand* continues to stir the hearts of readers with its arousing message. Although through successive editions the book has been slightly expanded, all the source material dates from a single period—the spacious days of evangelistic witness in China just prior to the Japanese war, when the author and his fellow Christians enjoyed a liberty in the service of God that is rare today. A message which expresses at once their triumphant assurance in the finished work of Christ and their humble sense of the high qualities called for in His servants has a fresh relevance for us now, when Christian work everywhere is on trial. May God give us grace not only to heed its challenge, but to find ways, while there is time, of applying its lessons in our own sphere of opportunity.

Angus I. Kinnear
London, 1962

Introduction

IF THE LIFE of a Christian is to be pleasing to God, it must be properly adjusted to Him in all things. Too often we place the emphasis in our own lives upon the application of this principle to some single detail of our behavior or of our work for Him. Often we fail therefore to appreciate either the extent of the adjustment called for or, at times even, the point from which it should begin.

But God measures everything, from start to finish, by the perfections of His Son. Scripture clearly affirms that it is God's good pleasure "to sum up all things in Christ, . . . in whom also we were made a heritage" (Eph. 1:9–11). It is my earnest prayer that, in the discussion that follows, our eyes may be opened afresh to see that it is only by placing our entire emphasis *there* that we can hope to realize the divine purpose for us, which is that "we should be unto the praise of his glory" (1:12).

We shall take as a background to our thoughts the epistle of Paul to the Ephesians.

Like so many of the apostle's letters, this epistle falls naturally into two sections: a doctrinal and a practical. The doctrinal section (chapters 1–3) is concerned mainly with the great facts of the redemption which God has wrought for us in Christ. The practical section (chapters 4–6) then goes on to present us with the demands, in terms of Christian conduct and zeal, that God is making upon us in the light of that redemption. The two halves are closely related, but it will be seen that the emphasis in each is different.

Then, further, the second and more obviously practical half of the letter may again conveniently be subdivided according to its subject matter into a first long section from verses 4:1 to 6:9 and a second, much shorter section from verse 6:10 to the end. The first part deals with our life in the midst of the world; the second with our conflict with the devil.

Thus, we have, in all, three subdivisions of the epistle to the Ephesians, setting forth the believer's position in Christ (1:1–3:21), his life in the world (4:1–6:9) and his attitude to the Enemy (6:10–24). We may summarize as follows:

Ephesians

    A. Doctrinal (Chapters 1 to 3)
        1. Our Position in Christ (1:1–3:21)
    B. Practical (Chapters 4 to 6)
        2. Our Life in the World (4:1–6:9)
        3. Our Attitude to the Enemy (6:10–24)

Of all Paul's epistles, it is in Ephesians that we find the highest spiritual truths concerning the Christian life. The letter abounds with spiritual riches, and yet at the same time it is intensely practical. The first half of the letter reveals our life in Christ to be one of union with Him in the highest heavens. The second half shows us in very practical terms how such a heavenly life is to be lived by us down here on the earth. We do not here propose to study the letter in detail. We shall, however, touch on a few principles lying at its heart. For this purpose we shall select one keyword in each of the above three sections to express what we believe to be its central or governing idea.

In the first section of the letter, we note the word "sit" (2:6), which is the key to that section and the secret of a true Christian experience. God has made us to sit with Christ in the heavenly places, and every Christian must begin his spiritual life from that place of rest. In the second part we select the word "walk" (4:1) as expressive of our life in the world, which is its subject. We are challenged there to display in our Christian walk conduct that is in keeping with our high calling. And finally, in the third part we find the key to our attitude toward the Enemy contained in the one word "stand" (6:11), expressive of our place of triumph at the end. Thus, we have:

KEY WORDS IN EPHESIANS
    1. Our Position in Christ—"SIT" (2:6)
    2. Our Life in the World—"WALK" (4:1)
    3. Our Attitude to the Enemy—"STAND" (6:11)

The life of the believer always presents these three aspects—to God, to man and to the Satanic powers. To be useful in God's hand, a man must be properly adjusted with respect to all three: his position, his life and his warfare. He falls short of God's requirements if he underestimates the importance of any one of them, for each is a sphere in which God would express "the glory of his grace, which he freely bestowed on us in the Beloved" (1:6).

We will take, then, these three words—"Sit," "Walk," "Stand"—as guides to the teaching of the epistle and as the text for its present message to our hearts. We shall find it most instructive to note both the order and the connection in which they come.

Chapter 1

Sit

"*THE GOD of our Lord Jesus Christ, . . . raised him from the dead, and made him to sit at his right hand in the heavenly places, far above all rule, and authority, and power, and dominion, and every name that is named, not only in this world, but also in that which is to come*" (1:17–21).

"*And raised us up with him, and made us to sit with him in the heavenly places, in Christ Jesus: . . . for by grace have ye been saved through faith; and that not of yourselves, it is the gift of God; not of works, that no man should glory*" (2:6–9).

"God . . . made him to sit . . . and made us to sit with him." Let us first consider the implications of this word "sit." As we have said, it reveals the secret of a heavenly life. Christianity does not begin with walking; it begins with sitting. The Christian era began with Christ, of whom we are told that, when He had made purification of sins, He "sat down on the right hand of the Majesty on high" (Heb. 1:3). With equal truth we can say that the individual Christian life begins with a man "in Christ"—that is to say, when by faith we see ourselves seated together with Him in the heavens.

Most Christians make the mistake of trying to walk in order to be able to sit, but that is a reversal of the true order. Our natural reason says, If we do not walk, how can we ever reach the goal? What can we attain without effort? How can we ever get anywhere if we do not move?

But Christianity is a queer business! If at the outset we try to do anything, we get nothing; if we seek to attain something, we miss everything. For Christianity begins not with a big DO, but with a big DONE. Thus, Ephesians opens with the statement that God *has* "blessed us with every spiritual blessing in the heavenly places in Christ" (1:3), and we are invited at the very outset to sit down and enjoy what God has done for us—not to set out to try and attain it for ourselves.

Walking implies effort, whereas God says that we are saved, not by works, but "by grace . . . through faith" (2:8). We constantly speak of being "saved through faith," but what do we mean by it? We mean this: that we are saved by reposing in the Lord Jesus. We did nothing whatever to save ourselves; we simply laid upon Him the burden of our sin-sick souls. We began our Christian life by depending not upon our own doing, but upon what He had done. Until a man does this, he is no Christian. For to say, "I can do nothing to save myself; but by His grace God *has done* everything for me in Christ," is to take the first step in the life of faith.

The Christian life from start to finish is based upon this principle of utter dependence upon the Lord Jesus. There is no limit to the grace God is willing to bestow upon us. He will give us everything, but we can receive none of it except as we rest in Him. "Sitting" is an attitude of rest. Something has been finished, work stops and we sit. It is paradoxical, but true, that we only advance in the Christian life as we learn first of all to sit down.

What does it really mean to sit down? When we walk or stand, we bear on our legs all the weight of our own body; but when we sit down, our entire weight rests upon the chair or couch on which we sit. We grow weary when we walk or stand, but we feel rested when we have sat down for awhile. In walking or standing we expend a great deal of energy, but when we are seated we relax at once, because the strain no longer falls upon our muscles and nerves, but upon something outside of ourselves. So also in the spiritual realm, to sit down is simply to rest our whole weight—our load, ourselves, our future, everything—upon the Lord. We let Him bear the responsibility and cease to carry it ourselves.

This was God's principle from the beginning. In the creation God worked from the first to the sixth day and rested on the seventh. We may truthfully say that for those first six days, He was very busy. Then, the task He had set Himself completed, He ceased to work. The seventh day became the sabbath of God; it was God's rest.

But what of Adam? Where did he stand in relation to that rest of God? Adam, we are told, was created on the sixth day. Clearly, then, he had no part in those first six days of work, for he came into being only at their end. God's seventh day was, in fact, Adam's first. Whereas God worked six days and then enjoyed His sabbath rest, Adam began his life with the sabbath; for God works before He rests, while man must first enter into God's rest, and then alone can he work.

Moreover, it was because God's work of creation was truly complete that Adam's life could begin with rest. And here is the gospel: that God has gone one stage further and has completed also the work of redemption, and that we need do nothing whatever to merit it, but can enter by faith directly into the values of His finished work.

Of course, we know that between these two historic facts—between God's rest in creation and God's rest in redemption—there lies the whole tragic story of Adam's sin and judgment, of man's unceasing, unprofitable labor and of the coming of the Son of God to toil and to give Himself until the lost position was recovered. "My Father worketh even until now, and I work" (John 5:17), He explained as He pursued His way. Only with the atoning price paid could He cry, "It is finished" (John 19:30).

But because of that triumphant cry, the analogy we have drawn is a true one. Christianity indeed means that God has done everything in Christ, and that we simply step by faith into the enjoyment of that fact. Our keyword here is not of course, in its context, a command to "sit down," but to see ourselves as "seated" in Christ. Paul prays that the eyes of our heart may be enlightened (1:18) to understand all that is contained for us in this double fact, that God has first by mighty power "made him to sit" and then by grace "made us to sit with him."

And the first lesson we must learn is this: that the work is not initially ours at all, but His. It is not that we work for God, but that He works for us. God *gives* us our position of rest. He brings His Son's finished work and presents it to us, and then He says to us, "Please sit" (*ch'eng tso*). His offer to us cannot, I think, be better expressed than in the words of the invitation to the great banquet: "Come; for all things are now ready" (Luke 14:17). Our Christian life begins with the discovery of what God has provided.

The Range of His Finished Work

From this point onward Christian experience proceeds as it began, not on the basis of our own work, but always on that of the finished work of Another. Every new spiritual experience begins with an acceptance by faith of what God has done—with a new "sitting down," if you like. This is a principle of life, and one which God Himself has appointed; and from beginning to end, each successive stage of the Christian life follows on the same divinely determined principle.

How can I receive the power of the Spirit for service? Must I labor for it? Must I plead with God for it? Must I afflict my soul by fastings and self-denials to merit it? Never! That is not the teaching of Scripture. Think again: How did we receive the forgiveness of our sins? Paul tells us that it was "according to the riches of his grace" (1:7), and that this was "freely bestowed on us in the Beloved" (1:6). We did nothing to merit it. We have our redemption through His blood, that is, on the ground of what *He* has done.

What then is God's basis for the outpouring of the Spirit? It is the exaltation of the Lord Jesus (Acts 2:33). Because Jesus died on the cross, my sins are forgiven; because He is exalted to the throne, I am endued with power from on high. The one gift is no more dependent than the other upon what I am or what I do. I did not merit forgiveness, and neither do I merit the gift of the Spirit. I receive everything not by walking, but by sitting down; not by doing, but by resting in the Lord.

Hence, just as there is no need to wait for the initial experience of salvation, so there is no need to wait for the Spirit's outpouring. Let me assure you that you need not plead with God for this gift, nor agonize, nor hold "tarrying meetings." It is yours not because of your doing, but because of the exaltation of Christ, "in whom, having also believed, ye were sealed with the Holy Spirit of promise." This, no less than the forgiveness of sins, is contained in "the gospel of your salvation" (1:13).

Or consider another subject, one that is a special theme of Ephesians. How do we become members of Christ? What fits us to be parts of that body which Paul speaks of as "the fulness of him"(1:23)? Certainly we never arrive there by walking. I am not joined to Him by effort of my own. "There is one body, and one Spirit, even as also ye were called in one hope of your calling" (4:4). Ephesians sets forth what *is*. It starts with Jesus Christ and with the fact that God chose us "*in him* before the foundation of the world" (1:4). When the Holy Spirit shows us Christ, and we believe on Him, then at once, with no further act on our part, there begins for us a life in union with Him.

But if all these things become ours by faith alone, what then of the now very urgent and practical matter of our sanctification? How can we know present deliverance from sin's reign? How is our "old man," who has followed us and troubled us for years, to be "crucified" and put away? Once again the secret is not in walking, but in sitting; not in doing, but in resting in something done. We "*died* to sin." We "*were baptized . . .* into his death." "We *were buried . . .* with him." God "*made us alive* together with Christ." (Rom. 6:2–4; Eph. 2:5).

All these statements are in the past (aorist) tense. Why is this? Because the Lord Jesus was crucified outside Jerusalem nearly two thousand years ago, and *I was crucified with Him.* This is the great historic fact. By it His experience has now become my spiritual history, and God can speak of me as already having everything "with him." All that I now have I have "with Christ." In the Scriptures we never find these things spoken of as in the future, nor even to be desired in the present. They are historic facts of Christ into which all we who have believed have entered.

"With Christ"—crucified, quickened, raised, set in the heavenlies. To the human mind these ideas are no less puzzling than were the words of Jesus to Nicodemus in John 3:3. There it was a question of how to be born again. Here it is something even more improbable—something not only to be effected in us, as new birth, but to be seen and accepted as ours because it *has already been effected* long ago in Someone else. How could such a thing be? We cannot explain. We must receive it from God as something He has done. We were not born with Christ, but we were crucified with Him (Gal. 2:20). Our union with Him began therefore with His death. God included us in Him there. We were "with him" because we were "in him."

But how can I be sure that I am "in Christ"? I can be sure because the Bible affirms that it is so, and that it was God who put me there. "Of him [God] are ye in Christ Jesus" (1 Cor. 1:30). "He that establisheth us with you in Christ . . . is God" (2 Cor. 1:21). It is something accomplished by Him in His sovereign wisdom to be seen, believed, accepted and rejoiced in by us.

If I put a dollar bill between the pages of a magazine and

then burn the magazine, where is the dollar bill? It has gone the same way as the magazine—to ashes. Where the one goes, the other goes too. Their history has become one. But just as effectively God has put us in Christ. What happened to Him happened also to us. All the experiences He met, we too have met *in Him*. "Our old man was crucified with him, that the body of sin might be done away, that so we should no longer be in bondage to sin" (Rom. 6:6).

That is not an exhortation to struggle. That is history— our history, written in Christ before we were born. Do you believe that? It is true! Our crucifixion with Christ is a glorious historic fact. Our deliverance from sin is based not on what we can do, nor even on what God is going to do for us, but on what He has already done for us in Christ. When that fact dawns upon us, and we rest back upon it (Rom. 6:11), then we have found the secret of a holy life.

But it is true that we know all too little of this in experience. Consider an example. If someone makes a very unkind remark about you in your presence, how do you meet the situation? You compress your lips, clench your teeth, swallow hard and take a firm grip upon yourself. And if with a great effort you manage to suppress all sign of resentment and be reasonably polite in return, you feel you have gained a great victory. But the resentment is still there; it has merely been covered up. And at times you do not even succeed in covering it.

What is the trouble? The trouble is that you are trying to walk before you have sat down, and in that way lies sure defeat. Let me repeat: No Christian experience begins with walking, but always with a definite sitting down. The secret of deliverance from sin is not to *do* something, but to rest on what God has done.

An engineer living in a large city in the West left his homeland for the Far East. He was away for two or three years, and during his absence his wife was unfaithful to him and went off with one of his best friends. On his return home he found he had lost his wife, his two children and his best friend. At the close of a meeting which I was addressing, this grief-stricken man unburdened himself to me. "Day and night for two solid years my heart has been full of hatred," he said. "I am a Christian, and I know I ought to forgive my wife and my friend, but though I try and try to forgive them, I simply cannot. Every day I resolve to love them, and every day I fail. What can I do about it?"

"Do nothing at all," I replied.

"What do you mean?" he asked, startled. "Am I to continue to hate them?"

So I explained, "The solution of your problem lies here, that when the Lord Jesus died on the cross, He not only bore your sins away, but He bore *you* away too. When He was crucified, your old man was crucified in Him, so that that unforgiving 'you,' who simply cannot love those who have wronged you, has been taken right out of the way in His death. God has dealt with the whole situation in the cross, and there is nothing left for you to deal with. Just say to Him, 'Lord, I cannot love, and I give up trying, but I count on Thy perfect love. I cannot forgive, but I trust Thee to forgive instead of me, and to do so henceforth in me.'"

The man sat there amazed and said, "That's all so new, I feel I must *do* something about it." Then a moment later he added again, "But what can I *do*?"

"God is waiting till you cease to do," I said. "When you cease doing, then God will begin. Have you ever tried to save a drowning man? The trouble is that his fear prevents him trusting himself to you. When that is so, there are just two ways of going about it. Either you must knock him unconscious and then drag him to the shore, or else you must leave him to struggle and shout until his strength gives way before you go to his rescue. If you try to save him while he has any strength left, he will clutch at you in his terror and drag you under, and both he and you will be lost. God is waiting for your store of strength to be utterly exhausted before He can deliver you. Once you have ceased to struggle, He will do everything. God is waiting for you to despair."

My engineer friend jumped up. "Brother," he said, "I've seen it. Praise God, it's all right now with me! There's nothing for me to do. *He* has done it all!" And with radiant face he went off rejoicing.

God the Giver

Of all the parables in the Gospels, that of the prodigal son affords, I think, the supreme illustration of the way to please God. The father says, "It was meet to make merry and be glad" (Luke 15:32), and in these words Jesus reveals what it is that, in the sphere of redemption, supremely rejoices His Father's heart. It is not an elder brother who toils incessantly for the father, but a younger brother who lets the father do everything for him. It is not an elder brother who always wants to be the giver, but a younger brother who is always willing to be the receiver. When the prodigal returned home, having wasted his substance in riotous living, the father had not a word of rebuke for the waste nor a word of inquiry regarding the substance. He did not sorrow over all that was spent; he only rejoiced over the opportunity the son's return afforded him for spending more.

God is so wealthy that His chief delight is to give. His treasure stores are so full that it is painful to Him when we refuse Him an opportunity of lavishing those treasures upon us. It was the father's joy that he could find in the prodigal an applicant for the robe, the ring, the shoes and the feast; it was his sorrow that in the elder son he found no such applicant.

It is a grief to the heart of God when we try to provide things for Him. He is so very, very rich. It gives Him true joy when we just let Him give and give and give again to us. It is a grief to Him, too, when we try to *do* things for Him, for He is so very, very able. He longs that we will just let Him do and do and do. He wants to be the Giver eternally, and He wants to be the Doer eternally. If only we saw how rich and how great He is, we would leave all the giving and all the doing to Him.

Do you think that if you cease trying to please God, your good behavior will cease? If you leave all the giving and all the working to God, do you think the result will be less satisfactory than if you do some of it? It is when we seek to do it ourselves that we place ourselves back again under the Law. But the works of the Law, even our best efforts, are "dead works," hateful to God because ineffectual.

In the parable both sons were equally far removed from the joys of the father's house. True, the elder son was not in the far country, yet he was only at home in theory. "These many years do I serve thee, and yet . . ." (Luke 15:29)—his heart had not found rest. His theoretical position could never, as did the prodigal's, come to be enjoyed by him while he still clung to his own good works.

Just you stop "giving," and you will prove what a Giver God is! Stop "working," and you will discover what a Worker He is! The younger son was all wrong, but he came home, and he found rest—and that is where Christian life begins. "God, being rich in mercy, for his great love wherewith he loved us . . . made us to sit with him in the heavenly places, in Christ Jesus" (Eph. 2:4, 6). "It was meet to make merry and be glad!" (Luke 15:32).

Chapter 2

Walk

WE HAVE sought to make it clear that Christian experience does not begin with walking, but with sitting. Every time we reverse the divine order, the result is disaster. The Lord Jesus has done everything for us, and our need now is to rest confidently in Him. He is seated on the throne, so we are carried through in His strength. It cannot be too strongly emphasized that all true spiritual experience begins from rest.

But it does not end there. Though the Christian life begins with sitting, sitting is always followed by walking. When once we have been well and truly seated and have found our strength in sitting down, then we do in fact begin to walk. Sitting describes our position with Christ in the heavenlies. Walking is the practical outworking of that heavenly position here on earth. As a heavenly people, we are required to bear the stamp of that heavenliness upon us in our earthly conduct, and this raises new problems. What then, we must now ask, has Ephesians to say to us about walking? We shall find that the epistle urges upon us two things. We will look now at the first of them.

"I therefore, the prisoner in the Lord, beseech you to walk worthily of the calling wherewith ye were called, with all lowliness and meekness . . ." (4:1–2).

"This I say . . . that ye no longer walk as the Gentiles also walk, in the vanity of their mind" . . . *But . . . "that ye be renewed in the spirit of your mind "* (4:17, 23).

"Walk in love, even as Christ also loved you, and gave himself up for us" (5:2).

"Walk as children of light, . . . proving what is well-pleasing unto the Lord " (5:8–10).

Eight times in Ephesians the word "walk" is used. It means literally "to walk around" and is used here figuratively by Paul to mean "to comport oneself; to order one's behavior." It brings immediately before us the subject of Christian conduct, and the second section of the letter is largely taken up with this.

But we saw earlier that the body of Christ, the fellowship of Christian believers, is another great theme of Ephesians. Now, here in chapter 4, it is in view of such fellowship that we find this matter of a holy walk arises. Paul proceeds, in the light of our heavenly calling, to challenge us upon the whole field of our relationships, both domestic and public, addressing himself to neighbors, to husbands and wives, to parents and children, employers and employed, all in a most realistic way.

Let us be clear that the body of Christ is not something remote and unreal, to be expressed only in heavenly terms. It is very present and practical, finding the real test of our conduct in our relations with others. For while it is true we are a heavenly people, it is no use just to talk of a distant heaven. Unless we bring heavenliness into our dwellings and offices, our shops and kitchens, and practice it there, it will be without meaning.

May I suggest this, dear friends, that those who are parents and those who are children look through the New Testament to see what parents should be and children should be? We may be surprised, for I fear many of us who say we are seated in the heavenlies in Christ display a very questionable walk in our homes. And husbands too, and wives—there are quite a number of passages for them. Read Ephesians 5 and then turn to First Corinthians 7. It would do every husband and every wife good to read the latter chapter carefully to discover what a real married life—a spiritual one before God and not just in theory—demands. You dare not theorize about a thing that is so practical.

Look now, in the field of Christian relationships, how forth-right are the commands of God in the section here before us. "Walk . . . with longsuffering, forbearing one another." "Putting away falsehood, speak ye truth each one with his neighbor." "Be ye angry, and sin not." "Steal no more." "Let all bitterness . . . be put away from you." "Be ye kind . . . forgiving each other." "Subjecting yourselves to one another." "Provoke not." "Be obedient." "Forbear threatening" (see Eph. 4–6). Nothing could be more realistic than this list of imperatives.

Let me remind you that the Lord Jesus Himself begins His teaching on this very note. Notice carefully the wording of this passage from His Sermon on the Mount: "Ye have heard that it was said, An eye for an eye, and a tooth for a tooth: but

I say unto you, resist not him that is evil: but whosoever smiteth thee on thy right cheek, turn to him the other also. And if any man would go to law with thee, and take away thy coat, let him have thy cloak also. And whosoever shall compel thee to go one mile, go with him two. Give to him that asketh thee, and from him that would borrow of thee turn not thou away. Ye have heard that it was said, Thou shalt love thy neighbor, and hate thine enemy: but I say unto you, love your enemies, and pray for them that persecute you; that ye may be sons of your Father who is in heaven: for he maketh his sun to rise on the evil and the good, and sendeth rain on the just and the unjust. For if ye love them that love you, what reward have ye? do not even the publicans the same? And if ye salute your brethren only, what do ye more than others? do not even the Gentiles the same? Ye therefore shall be perfect, as your heavenly Father is perfect" (Matt. 5:38–48).

"But," you say, "I cannot do it. These are impossible demands." Maybe, like my engineer friend, you feel you have been wronged—perhaps terribly wronged—and you cannot bring yourself to forgive. *You* were in the right, and your enemy's action has been wholly unjust. To love him may be ideal, but it is impossible.

The Perfection of the Father

Since the day that Adam took the fruit of the tree of knowledge, man has been engaged in deciding what is good and what is evil. The natural man has worked out his own standards of right and wrong, justice and injustice, and striven to live by them. Of course, as Christians, we are different. Yes, but in what way are we different? Since we were converted, a new sense of righteousness has been developed in us, with the result that we too, quite rightly, are occupied with the question of good and evil. But have we realized that for us the starting point is a different one? Christ is for us the Tree of Life. We do not begin from the matter of ethical right and wrong. We do not start from that other tree. We begin from *Him*; and the whole question for us is one of life.

Nothing has done greater damage to our Christian testimony than our trying to be right and demanding right of others. We become preoccupied with what is and what is not right. We ask ourselves, Have we been justly or unjustly treated? and we think thus to vindicate our actions. But that is not our standard. The whole question for us is one of cross-bearing.

You ask me, "Is it right for someone to strike my cheek?" I reply, "Of course not!" But the question is, do you only want to be right? As Christians, our standard of living can never be "right or wrong," but the cross. The principle of the cross is our principle of conduct. Praise God that He makes His sun to shine on the evil and the good. With Him it is a question of His grace and not of right or wrong. But that is to be our standard also: "Forgiving each other, even as God also in Christ forgave you" (4:32). "Right or wrong" is the principle of the Gentiles and tax gatherers. My life is to be governed by the principle of the cross and of the perfection of the Father: "Ye therefore shall be perfect, as your heavenly Father is perfect" (Matt. 5:48).

A brother in South China had a rice field in the middle of the hill. In time of drought, he used a waterwheel worked by a treadmill to lift water from the irrigation stream into his field. His neighbor had two fields below his, and one night made a breach in the dividing bank and drained off all his water. When the brother repaired the breach and pumped in more water, his neighbor did the same thing again, and this was repeated three or four times. So he consulted his brethren. "I have tried to be patient and not to retaliate," he said, "but *is it right?*" After they had prayed together about it, one of them replied, "If we only try to do the right thing, surely we are very poor Christians. We have to do something more than what is right." The brother was much impressed. Next morning he pumped water for the two fields below, and in the afternoon pumped water for his own field. After that the water stayed in his field. His neighbor was so amazed at his action that he began to inquire the reason, and in course of time, he too became a Christian.

So, my brethren, don't stand on your right. Don't feel that because you have gone the second mile you have done what is just. The second mile is only typical of the third and the fourth. The principle is that of conformity to Christ. We have nothing to stand for, nothing to ask or demand. We have only to give. When the Lord Jesus died on the cross, He did not do so to defend our "rights"; it was grace that took Him there. Now, as His children, we try always to give others what is their due and more.

We have to remind ourselves that we are often *not* right. We fail, and it is always good to learn from our failures—to be ready to confess and willing to go beyond what is necessary in doing so. The Lord wants this. Why? "That ye may be sons of your Father who is in heaven" (Matt. 5:45). The question is one of practical sonship. True, God has "foreordained us unto adoption as sons through Jesus Christ" (1:5), but we make the mistake of thinking that we have already "come of age"—that we are already mature sons. The Sermon on the Mount teaches us that the children attain to the responsibility of sons in the measure in which they manifest kinship of spirit and of attitude with their Father. We are called to be "perfect" in love, showing forth His grace. So Paul also writes, "Be ye therefore imitators of God, as beloved children; and walk in love, even as Christ also loved you, and gave himself up for us" (5:1–2).

We are faced with a challenge. Matthew 5 sets a standard that we may well feel is impossibly high, and Paul in this section of Ephesians endorses it. The trouble is that we just do not find in ourselves by nature the means to attain to that standard—to walk "as becometh saints" (5:3). Where then lies the answer to our problem of God's exacting demands?

The secret is, in the words of Paul, "the power that worketh in us" (3:20). In a parallel passage (Col. 1:29) he says: "I labor also, striving according to his working, which worketh in me mightily."

We are back again in the first section of Ephesians. What is the secret strength of the Christian life? From where does it derive its power? Let me give you the answer in a sentence: *The Christian's secret is his rest in Christ.* His power derives from his God-given position. All who sit can walk, for in the thought of God, the one follows the other spontaneously. We sit forever with Christ that we may walk continuously before men. Forsake for a moment our place of rest in Him, and immediately we are tripped, and our testimony in the world is marred. But abide in Christ, and our position there ensures the power to walk worthy of Him here.

If you desire an illustration of this kind of progress, think first of all not of a runner in a race, but of a man in a car or, better still, of a cripple in a power-driven invalid carriage.

What does he do? He *goes*—but he also *sits*. And he keeps going because he remains sitting. His progress follows from the position in which he has been placed. This, of course, is a far from perfect picture of the Christian life, but it may serve to remind us that our conduct and behavior depend fundamentally upon our inward rest in Christ.

This explains Paul's language here. He has first learned to sit. He has come to a place of rest in God. As a result, his walking is not based on his efforts but on God's mighty inward working. There lies the secret of his strength. Paul has seen himself seated in Christ; therefore his walk before men takes its character from Christ dwelling in him. Small wonder that he prays for the Ephesians "that Christ may dwell in your hearts through faith" (3:17).

How does my wristwatch go? By moving first, or by being moved? Of course it goes because first it is moved by a power outside itself. Then only will it do the work for which it was designed. And there are works for which we too are designed. "We are his workmanship, created in Christ Jesus for good works, which God afore prepared that we should walk in them" (2:10). "Work out your own salvation with fear and trembling," writes Paul to the Philippians, "for it is God who worketh in you both to will and to work, for his good pleasure" (2:12–13). God is working it in; work it out! That is the secret.

But until we are willing for God to work it in, it is useless for us to try to work it out. Often we try to be meek and gentle without knowing what it means to let God work in us the meekness and gentleness *of Christ*. We try to show love, and, finding we have none, we ask the Lord for love. Then we are surprised that He does not seem to give it to us.

Let me take up again an earlier illustration. Perhaps there is a certain brother whom you find very trying and with whom you are constantly getting into difficulties. Whenever you meet him, he says or does something calculated to arouse in you resentment. This troubles you. You say, "I am a Christian and ought to love him! I want to love him; indeed I am *determined* to love him!" And so you pray very earnestly, "Lord, increase my love for him. O God, give me love!" Then, taking a firm grip on yourself and summoning all your will-power, you set out with a genuine desire to display to him that love for which you have prayed. But alas, when you get into his presence, something happens to bring all your good intentions to nought. His response to you is not in the least encouraging, but rather the reverse, and immediately your old resentment flares up; and once again the utmost you can do is to be polite to him.

Why is this? You were surely not *wrong* in seeking love from God? No, but you were wrong in seeking that love as something in itself, a kind of package commodity, when what God desires is to express through you the love of His Son.

God has given us Christ. There is nothing now for us to receive outside of Him. The Holy Spirit has been sent to produce what is of Christ in us; not to produce anything that is apart from or outside of Him. We are "strengthened with power through his Spirit in the inward man; . . . to know the love of Christ" (3:16, 19). What we show forth outwardly is what God has first put within.

Recall once again the great words of First Corinthians 1:30. Not only did God set us "in Christ." By Him also "Christ Jesus . . . was made unto us wisdom from God, and righteousness and sanctification, and redemption." This is one of the grandest statements in Scripture. *He* "was made unto us. . . ." If we believe this, we can put in there anything we need and can know that God has made it good; for through the Holy Spirit within us, the Lord Jesus is Himself made unto us whatever we lack. We have been accustomed to look upon holiness as a virtue, upon humility as a grace, upon love as a gift to be sought from God. But the Christ of God is *Himself* everything that we shall ever need.

Many a time in my need I used to think of Christ as a Person apart, and failed to identify Him in this practical way with the "things" I felt so strongly the lack of. For two whole years I was groping in that kind of darkness, seeking to amass the virtues that I felt sure should make up the Christian life, and getting nowhere in the effort. And then one day—it was in the year 1933—light broke from heaven for me, and I saw Christ ordained of God to be made over to me in His fullness. What a difference! Oh the emptiness of "things"! Held by us out of relation to Christ, they are dead. Once we see this, it will be the beginning of a new life for us. Our holiness will be spelled thereafter with a capital H, our love with a capital L. *He Himself* is revealed as the answer in us to all God's demands.

Go back now to that difficult brother, but this time, before you go, address God thus: "Lord, it is clear to me at last that in myself I cannot love him at all; but I know now that there is a life within me, the life of thy Son, and that the law of that life is to love. It cannot but love him." There is no need to exert yourself. Repose in Him. Count upon His life. Dare thus to go and see that brother and to speak to him—and here is the amazing thing! Quite unconsciously (and I would emphasize the word "unconsciously," for the consciousness only comes afterwards) you find yourself speaking most pleasantly to him; quite unconsciously you love him; quite unconsciously you know him as your brother. You converse with him freely and in true fellowship, and on your return you find yourself saying with amazement, "Why, I did not exercise the least bit of anxious care just now, and yet I did not become in the least bit irritable! In some unaccountable way the Lord was with me, and His love triumphed."

The operation of His life in us is in a true sense spontaneous, that is to say, it is without effort of ours. The all-important rule is not to "try," but to "trust," not to depend upon our own strength, but upon His. For it is the flow of life which reveals what we truly are "in Christ." It is from the Fountain of Life that the sweet water issues.

Too many of us are caught *acting* as Christians. The life of many Christians today is largely a pretense. They live a "spiritual" life, talk a "spiritual" language, adopt "spiritual" attitudes, but they are doing the whole thing themselves. It is the effort involved that should reveal to them that something is wrong. They force themselves to refrain from doing this, from saying that, from eating the other—and how hard they find it all! It is just the same as when we Chinese try to talk a language that is not our own. No matter how hard we try, it does not come spontaneously; we have to force ourselves to talk that way. But when it comes to speaking our own language, nothing could be easier. Even when we forget all about what we are doing, we still speak it. It flows. It comes to us perfectly naturally, and its very spontaneity reveals to everyone *what we are*.

Our life *is* the life of Christ, mediated in us by the indwelling Holy Spirit Himself, and the law of that life *is* spontaneous. The moment we see that fact, we shall end our struggling and cast away our pretense. Nothing is so hurtful to the life of a Christian as acting; nothing so blessed as when our outward efforts cease and our attitudes become natural—when our words, our prayers, our very life all become a spontaneous and unforced expression of the life within. Have we discovered how good the Lord is? Then *in us* He is as good as that! Is His power great? Then *in us* it is no less great! Praise God, His life is as mighty as ever, and in the lives of those who dare to believe the Word of God, the divine life will be manifest in a power not one whit less mighty than was manifest of old.

What does our Lord mean when He says, "Except your righteousness shall exceed the righteousness of the scribes and Pharisees, ye shall in no wise enter into the kingdom of heaven"? (Matt. 5:20). We have seen above how He goes on to set the contrast between the requirements of the Law of Moses and His own tremendous demands by His repeated use of the words "Ye have heard that it was said . . . but I say unto you. . . ." (Matt. 5). But since already, over many centuries, men had sought to attain to the first standard and had failed, how could the Lord dare to raise the standard higher still? He could do so only because He believed in His own life. He is not afraid of making the most exacting demands upon Himself. Indeed, we may well find comfort in reading the laws of the Kingdom as set forth in Matthew chapters 5 to 7, for they show what utter confidence the Lord has in His own life *made available to His children*. These three chapters set forth the divine taxation of the divine life. The greatness of His demands upon us only shows how confident He is that the resources He has put within us are fully enough to meet them.

God does not command what He will not perform; but we must throw ourselves back on Him for the performance.

Does some difficult situation confront us? Is it a problem of right or wrong, good or evil? We do not need to look for wisdom. We need no longer apply to the tree of knowledge. We have Christ, and *He* is made unto us wisdom from God. The law of the Spirit of life in Christ Jesus continually communicates to us His standards of right and wrong, and with them the attitude of spirit with which the difficult situation should be met.

More and more things will turn up to hurt our Christian sense of righteousness and to test what our reactions are going to be. We need to learn the principle of the cross—that our standard is not now the old, but the new man, "that after God hath been created in righteousness and holiness of truth" (4:24). "Lord, I've got no rights to defend. Everything I have is through Thy grace, and everything is in Thee!" I knew of an old Japanese Christian woman who was disturbed by a thief who had broken into her house. In her simple but practical faith in the Lord, she cooked the man a meal—then offered him her keys. He was shamed by her action, and God spoke to him. Through her testimony that man is a brother in Christ today.

Too many Christians have all the doctrine, but live lives that are a contradiction of it. They know all about chapters 1 to 3 of Ephesians, but they do not put chapters 4 to 6 into practice. It were better to have no doctrine than to be a contradiction. Has God commanded something? Then throw yourself back on God for the means to do what He has commanded. May the Lord teach us that the whole principle of the Christian life is that we go beyond what is right to do that which is well-pleasing to Him.

Redeeming the Time

But there remains something further to be added to the above on the subject of our Christian walk. The word "walk" has, as must already be obvious, a further meaning. It suggests first conduct or behavior, but it also contains in it the idea of progress. To "walk" is to "proceed," to "follow on," and we want to consider briefly now this further matter of our progress toward a goal.

"Look therefore carefully how ye walk, not as unwise, but as wise; redeeming the time, because the days are evil. Wherefore be ye not foolish, but understand what the will of the Lord is" (5:15–17).

You will notice that in the above verses there is an association between the idea of time and the difference between wisdom and foolishness. "Walk . . . as wise; redeeming the time . . . . Be ye not foolish." This is important. I want now to remind you of two other passages in which these things are similarly brought together.

"Then shall the kingdom of heaven be likened unto ten virgins . . . . Five of them were foolish, and five were wise. For the foolish, when they took their lamps, took no oil with them . . . . But at midnight there is a cry, Behold, the bridegroom! Come ye forth to meet him. Then all those virgins arose, and trimmed their lamps. And the foolish said . . . Our lamps are going out . . . . And while they went away to buy, the bridegroom came; and they that were ready went in with him to the marriage feast: and the door was shut. Afterward came also the other virgins . . . ." (Matt. 25:1–13).

"And I saw, and behold, the Lamb standing on the mount Zion, and with him a hundred and forty and four thousand, having his name, and the name of his Father, written on their foreheads. . . . They are virgins. These are they that follow the Lamb whithersoever he goeth. These were purchased from among men, to be the firstfruits unto God and unto the Lamb. And in their mouth was found no lie: they are without blemish" (Rev. 14:1–5).

There are many passages of Scripture that assure us that what God has begun, He will finish. Our Savior is a Savior to the uttermost. No Christian believer will be "half saved" at the end, even if now that might be said of us in any sense. God will perfect every man who has faith in Him. That is what we believe, and we must keep it in mind as a background for what we are going to say next. With Paul, we are "confident of this very thing, that he who began a good work in you will perfect it until the day of Jesus Christ" (Phil 1:6). There are no limits to God's power. He "is able . . . to set you before the presence of his glory without blemish" (Jude 24; see also 2 Tim. 1:12 and Eph. 3:20).

It is, however, when we turn to the subjective aspect of this—to its practical outworking in our lives here and now on the earth—that we encounter the question of time. In Revelation 14 there are firstfruits (v. 4), and there is a harvest (v. 15). What is the difference between harvest and firstfruits? It is certainly not one of quality, for the whole crop is one. Their difference lies only in the time of their ripeness. Some fruits reach maturity before others, and thus they become "firstfruits."

My home town in Fukien province is famous for its oranges. I would say (and no doubt I am prejudiced!) that there are none like them anywhere in the world. As you look out on the hills at the beginning of the orange season, all the groves are green. But if you look more carefully, you will see, sprinkled here and there on the trees, golden oranges already showing up. It is a beautiful sight to see the flecks of gold dotted among the dark green trees. Later the whole crop will ripen, and the groves will turn to gold, but now it is these firstfruits that are gathered. They are carefully handpicked, and it is they that fetch the top market prices—often three times the price of the harvest.

All will reach ripeness, somehow. But the Lamb is seeking firstfruits. The "wise" in the parable are not those who have done better, but those who have done well *at an earlier hour*. The others, be it noted, were also virgins—"foolish," no doubt, but not false. Along with the wise, they had gone out to meet the Bridegroom. They too had oil in their lamps, and their lamps were burning. But they had not reckoned on His tarrying, and now that their lamps burned low, they had no reserve of oil in their vessels, nor had the others enough to spare them.

Some are troubled at this point by the Lord's words to the foolish ones: "I know you not" (Matt. 25:12). How, they feel, could He say this of them if they represent His true children, "espoused . . . as a pure virgin to Christ"? (2 Cor. 11:2). But we must recognize the whole point of the teaching of this parable, which is surely that there is some privilege of serving Him in the future which His children may miss by being unprepared. It says that the five came to the door and said, "Lord, Lord, open to us" (Matt. 25:11). What door? Certainly not the door of salvation. If you are lost, you cannot come to the door of heaven and knock. When therefore the

Lord says, "I know you not," He surely uses these words in some such limited sense as in the following illustration.

In Shanghai the son of a police court magistrate was arrested for careless driving. He was brought to court and found his father sitting on the magistrate's bench. Court procedure is more or less the same the world over, and so the boy was asked, "What is your name? What is your address? What is your occupation?" and so on.

Astonished, he turned to his father. "Father, do you mean to say you don't know me?"

Rapping on his desk, the father answered sternly, "Young man, I do not know you. What is your name? What is your address?" He did not of course mean by this that he did not know him at all. In the family and in the home he knew him, but *in that place and at that time* he did not know him. Though still his father's son, the boy must go right through the court procedure and pay his fine.

Yes, all ten virgins had oil in their lamps. What distinguished the foolish was that they had no reserve in their vessels. As true Christians, they have life in Christ, and they have a testimony before men. But theirs is a fitful testimony, for they live a hand-to-mouth existence. They have the Spirit, but they are not, we may say, "filled with the Spirit." When the crisis comes, they must go out to buy more oil. In the end, of course, all the ten had enough. But the difference lay in the fact that the wise had sufficient oil in time, while the foolish, when at length they did have sufficient, had missed the purpose for which it was intended. It is all a question of time, and this is the point which the Lord seeks to drive home when, at the end of the parable, He urges His disciples not just to be disciples, but to be watchful disciples.

"Be not drunken with wine, wherein is riot, but be filled with the Spirit" (5:18). In Matthew 25 it is not a question of the initial reception of Jesus Christ, nor yet of the coming of the Holy Spirit upon His servants for spiritual gifts! It is a question of the extra oil in the vessel—of the light being sustained, through however long a time of waiting, by means of the continual miraculous supply of the Spirit within (for whereas in the parable there is both a lamp and a vessel, in reality we are the lamp, and we are the vessel).

What Christian could possibly live in eternity in heaven without knowing this inner fullness? Surely not one virgin can escape this? And so the Lord is taking all possible steps to bring us to the knowledge of that fullness now. "Watch therefore, for ye know not the day nor the hour" (Matt. 25:13).

"Be being filled" (*plerousthe*) is the unusual expression used here in relation to the Holy Spirit (see Eph. 5:18). "Allow yourselves to be continually made full." It is not a crisis, as at Pentecost, but a state we are to be in all the time. And it is not something external, but internal; not a question of spiritual gifts and manifestations outwardly, but of the personal presence and activity of the Holy Spirit within our spirits, guaranteeing that the light in the vessel will burn undimmed—long after midnight if need be.

And moreover, it is not wholly a personal thing. As the next verse (5:19) surely indicates, it is something which we share with other Christians in mutual dependence. For to be "filled with the Spirit" means, in the language of that verse, not merely "singing and making melody with your heart to the Lord," but "*speaking one to another* in psalms and hymns and spiritual songs." Some of us may well find it easy to sing solos, but much harder to sing in time and harmony as a quartet or even as a duet. Yet this message of oneness in the Spirit lies at the heart of our second section of Ephesians (see 4:3, 15–16). The fullness of the Spirit is given to us that we should sing *together* a new song before the throne (Rev. 14:3).

But, to keep to our main emphasis, let me repeat that folly or wisdom hinges on this one point alone: that if you are wise, you will seek this fullness sooner, but if you are foolish, you will put if off till later. Some of us are parents and have children. How greatly those children can differ in temperament! One will obey at once; another will think that by procrastination he can avoid the need to do so. If that is indeed the case, and you are weak enough to allow him a loophole for escape, then the one who procrastinates is in fact the wise one, for he succeeds in doing nothing. But if your word holds, if your command cannot be evaded and ultimately *must* be obeyed, then he is certainly the wiser who faces the issue squarely at once.

Get clear about the will of God. If God's words can be discounted, then you might not be foolish to try to escape their implications. But if God is an unchanging God with an unchanging will, then be wise; redeem the time. Seek above all things to have that extra supply of oil in the vessel, "that ye may be filled unto all the fulness of God" (3:19).

The parable does not answer all our questions. How do the foolish buy? We are not told. We are nowhere told what further steps God may have to take to bring all His children eventually to maturity. That is not our concern. We are concerned here with firstfruits. We are being urged to press on; not to speculate on what may happen if we don't.

You cannot, by dodging the issue, avoid reaching maturity—or paying the price of it. But wisdom is connected with time. Those who are wise redeem the time. Just as my fountain pen is now filled and ready to my hand for immediate use, so, by cooperating with the Lord, the wise provide God with what He wants: handy tools, instantly available to Him.

Look at the apostle Paul. He is consumed with a burning passion. He has seen that God's purpose for us is bound up with the "fulness of the times" (1:10). He is one of those who have "before hoped in Christ" by resting in a salvation that is yet to be fully revealed "in the ages to come" (1:12, 2:7). And in view of all this, what does he do? He walks. And he not only walks; he runs. "I therefore so run, as not uncertainly" (1 Cor. 9:26). "I press on toward the goal unto the prize of the high calling of God in Christ Jesus" (Phil. 3:14).

Often when souls come into an understanding of spiritual things and begin to go on with the Lord, the feeling in my heart is, "Oh, if only they had come to see this five years earlier!" The time is so short, even if we *are* going on. There is such need for urgency. For remember, it is not a question of what we get out of it. It is a question of *what the Lord must have now*. The Lord's need today is for ready instruments. Why? "Because the days are evil" (5:16). The situation is desperate among the Christian public. Oh, that we might see it!

The Lord may have to deal drastically with us. Paul had to say, "I am an abortive child." He had passed through tremendous crises to bring him to the point where he then was—and still he pressed on. It is always a question of time. God may have to do something in us swiftly, compressing it into a short space; but He *has* to do that much. May the eyes of our heart be enlightened to know what is "the hope of his calling," and then may we walk—nay, run—as those who "understand what the will of the Lord is" (1:18, 5:17). The Lord always loves desperate souls.

Chapter 3

Stand

"*FINALLY, BE STRONG in the Lord, and in the strength of his might. Put on the whole armor of God, that ye may be able to stand against the wiles of the devil. . . . That ye may be able to withstand in the evil day, and, having done all, to stand. Stand therefore, having girded your loins . . . having put on the breastplate . . . having shod your feet . . . taking up the shield. . . . And the helmet . . . and the sword . . . praying . . . and watching*" (6:10–11, 13–18).

Christian experience begins with sitting and leads to walking, but it does not end with these. Every Christian must learn also to stand. Each one of us must be prepared for the conflict. We must know how to sit with Christ in heavenly places, and we must know how to walk worthy of Him down here, but we must also know how to stand before the Foe. This matter of conflict now comes before us in the third section of Ephesians (6:10–20). It is what Paul calls our "wrestling" with wicked spirits.

But let us first remind ourselves once again of the order in which Ephesians presents us with these things. It is "sit . . . walk . . . stand." For no Christian can hope to enter the warfare of the ages without learning first to rest in Christ and in what He has done, and then, through the strength of the Holy Spirit within, to follow Him in a practical, holy life here on earth. If he is deficient in either of these, he will find that all the talk about spiritual warfare remains only talk; he will never know its reality. Satan can afford to ignore him, for he does not count for anything.

Yet the very same Christian can be made strong "in the Lord, and in the strength of his might" by knowing the values first of His exaltation and then of His indwelling (compare 6:10 with 1:19 and 3:16). It is with these two lessons well and truly learned that he comes to appreciate the third principle of the Christian life now summed up in the word "stand."

God has an archenemy, and under his power are countless demons and fallen angels seeking to overrun the world with evil and to exclude God from His own kingdom. This is the meaning of verse 12. It is an explanation of things taking place around us. *We* see only "flesh and blood" ranged against us—that is to say, a world system of hostile kings and rulers, sinners and evil men. No, says Paul, our wrestling is not against these, "but against the principalities, against the powers, against the world-rulers of this darkness, against the spiritual hosts of wickedness in the heavenly places"—in short, against the wiles of the devil himself.

Two thrones are at war. God is claiming the earth for His dominion, and Satan is seeking to usurp the authority of

God. The church is called to displace Satan from his present realm and to make Christ Head over all. What are we doing about it?

I want now to deal with this matter of our warfare—first in general terms in relation to our personal Christian lives and then in a more special sense in relation to the work of the Lord entrusted to us. There are many direct assaults of Satan upon God's children. Of course, we must not attribute to the devil those troubles that are the result of our own breach of divine laws. We should by now know how to put these right. But there are physical attacks upon the saints, attacks of the evil one upon their bodies and minds, of which we must take serious account. Surely too there are few of us who do not know something of the Enemy's assaults upon our spiritual life. Are we going to let these pass unchallenged?

We have our position with the Lord in the heavenlies, and we are learning how to walk with Him before the world; but how are we to acquit ourselves in the presence of the adversary—His adversary and ours? God's word is "stand"! "Put on the whole armor of God that you may be able to stand against the wiles of the devil." The Greek verb "stand" with its following preposition "against" in verse 11 really means "hold your ground."

There is a precious truth hidden in that command of God. It is not a command to invade a foreign territory. Warfare, in modern parlance, would imply a command to "march." Armies march into other countries to occupy and to subdue. God has not told us to do this. We are not to march, but to stand. The word "stand" implies that the ground disputed by the Enemy is really God's, and therefore ours. We need not struggle to gain a foothold on it.

Nearly all the weapons of our warfare described in Ephesians are purely defensive. Even the sword can be used as well for defense as for offense. The difference between defensive and offensive warfare is this: that in the former I have got the ground and only seek to keep it, whereas in the latter I have not got the ground and am fighting in order to get it. And that is precisely the difference between the warfare waged by the Lord Jesus and the warfare waged by us. His was offensive; ours is, in essence, defensive.

He warred against Satan in order to gain the victory. Through the cross He carried that warfare to the very threshold of hell itself, to lead forth from there His "captivity captive" (4:8–9). Today we war against Satan only to maintain and consolidate the victory which Christ has already gained. By the resurrection God proclaimed His Son victor over the whole realm of darkness, and the ground Christ won He has given to us. We do not need to fight to obtain it. We only need to hold it against all challengers.

Our task is one of holding, not of attacking. It is a matter not of advance, but of sphere—the sphere of Christ. In the person of Jesus Christ, God has already conquered. He has given us His victory to *hold*. Within the sphere of Christ, the Enemy's defeat is already a fact, and the church has been put there to keep him defeated. Satan is the one who must do the counterattacking in his efforts to dislodge us from that sphere.

For our part, we need not struggle to occupy ground that is already ours. In Christ we *are* conquerors—nay, "more than conquerors" (Rom. 8:37). In Him, therefore, we *stand*. Thus, today we do not fight *for* victory; we fight *from* victory. We do not fight in order to win, but because in Christ we have already won. Overcomers are those who rest in the victory already given to them by their God.

When you fight to *get* the victory, then you have lost the battle at the very outset. Suppose Satan sets out to assault you in your home or in your business. Difficulties mount up, misunderstandings arise, a situation that you can neither deal with nor escape threatens to overwhelm you. You pray, you fast, you struggle and resist for days, but nothing happens. Why? You are trying to fight into victory, and in doing so are relinquishing to the Enemy the very ground that is yours. For victory is still for you a distant thing, somewhere ahead of you, and you cannot reach it.

I was in just such a situation once myself, and God brought to my mind the word in Second Thessalonians concerning the man of sin, whom the Lord Jesus "shall slay with the breath of his mouth" (2:8). The thought came, *It will need but a breath from my Lord to finish him off, and here am I trying to raise a hurricane! Was not Satan once for all defeated? Then this victory too is already won.*

Only those who sit can stand. Our power for standing, as for walking, lies in our having first been made to sit together with Christ. The Christian's walk and warfare alike derive their strength from his position there. If he is not sitting before God, he cannot hope to stand before the Enemy.

Satan's primary object is not to get us to sin, but simply to make it easy for us to do so by getting us off the ground of perfect triumph onto which the Lord has brought us. Through the avenue of the head or of the heart, through our intellect or our feelings, he assaults our rest in Christ or our walk in the Spirit. But for every point of his attack, defensive armor is provided—the helmet and the breastplate, the girdle and the shoes—while over all is the shield of faith to turn aside his fiery darts. Faith says, Christ is exalted. Faith says, We are saved by His grace. Faith says, We have access through Him. Faith says, He indwells us by His Spirit (see 1:20; 2:8; 3:12, 17).

Because victory is His, therefore it is ours. If only we will not try to gain the victory, but simply to maintain it, then we shall see the Enemy utterly routed. We must not ask the Lord to enable *us* to overcome the Enemy, nor even look to *Him* to overcome, but praise Him because He has already done so; He *is* victor. It is all a matter of faith in Him. If we believe the Lord, we shall not pray so much, but rather we shall praise Him more. The simpler and clearer our faith in Him, the less we shall pray in such situations, and the more we shall praise.

Let me say again: In Christ we *are already* conquerors. Is it not obvious then, since this is so, that for us merely to pray for victory—unless that prayer is shot through with praise—must be to court defeat by throwing away our fundamental position?

Let me ask you: Has defeat been your experience? Have you found yourself hoping that one day you will be strong enough to win? Then my prayer for you can go no further than that of the apostle Paul to his Ephesian readers. It is that God may open your eyes anew to see yourself seated with Him who has Himself been made to sit "far above all rule, and authority, and power, and dominion, and every name that is named" (1:21). The difficulties around you may not alter; the lion may roar as loudly as ever; but you need no longer *hope* to overcome. In Christ Jesus you *are* victor in the field.

In His Name

But this is not all. Ephesians 6 is concerned with more than the personal side of our warfare. It has to do too with the work of God entrusted to us—the utterance of the mystery of the gospel of which Paul has already had much to say (see 3:1–13). For this it arms us now with the sword of the Word and its companion weapon, prayer.

"Take . . . the sword of the Spirit, which is the word of God: with all prayer and supplication praying at all seasons in the Spirit, and watching thereunto in all perseverance and supplication for all the saints, and on my behalf, that utterance may be given unto me in opening my mouth, to make known with boldness the mystery of the gospel, for which I am an ambassador in chains; that in it I may speak boldly, as I ought to speak" (6:17–20).

I want to say something more about this warfare in its relation to our work for God, for here we may encounter a difficulty. It is true, on the one hand, that our Lord Jesus is seated "far above all rule, and authority," and that all things have been put "in subjection under his feet" (1:21–22). Clearly it is in the light of this completed victory that we are to give "thanks always for all things *in the name of our Lord Jesus Christ*" (5:20).

Yet on the other hand, we have to admit that we do not yet see all things subject to Him. There are still, as Paul says, hosts of wicked spirits in the heavenly places—dark, evil powers behind this world's rulers, occupying territory that is rightly His. How far are we correct in calling this a defensive warfare?

We do not want to be falsely presumptive. When, therefore, and under what conditions are we justified in occupying territory that is outwardly the Enemy's and holding it in the name of the Lord Jesus?

Let us "take . . . the word of God" to help us here. What does it tell us about prayer and action "in the name"? Consider first the following two passages: "Verily I say unto you, what things soever ye shall bind on earth shall be bound in heaven; and what things soever ye shall loose on earth shall be loosed in heaven. Again I say unto you, that if two of you shall agree on earth as touching anything that they shall ask, it shall be done for them . . . . For where two or three are gathered together in my name, there am I. . . ." (Matt. 18:18–20). "In that day ye shall ask me no question. Verily, verily, I say unto you, if ye shall ask anything of the Father, he will give it you in my name. Hitherto have ye asked nothing in my name: ask, and ye shall receive, that your joy may be made full. . . . In that day ye shall ask in my name" (John 16:23–24, 26).

None can be saved without knowing the name of Jesus, and none can be effectively used of God without knowing the authority of that name. The apostle Paul makes it clear that the "name" to which Jesus alludes in the above passages is not simply the name by which He was known while here among men. To be sure, it *is* that very selfsame name of His humanity, but it is that name invested now with the title and authority given to Him by God after He had become obedient to death (Phil. 2:6–10). It is the outcome of His sufferings, the name of His exaltation and glory; and today it is in *that* "name which is above every name" that we gather and that we ask of God.

This distinction is made not by Paul alone, but already by Jesus Himself in the second passage quoted above: "Hitherto ye have asked nothing . . . . In that day ye shall ask" (verses 24, 26). For the disciples "that day" will differ greatly from the "now" of verse 22. Something they do not have now they will receive then, and having received it, they will use it. That something is the authority that goes with His name.

Our eyes must be opened to see the mighty change wrought by the ascension. The name of Jesus certainly establishes the identity of the One on the throne with the Carpenter of Nazareth, but it goes further than that. It represents now the power and dominion given to Him by God, a power and a dominion before which every knee in heaven and earth and beneath the earth must bow. Even the Jewish leaders recognized that there could be this kind of significance in a mere name when they inquired of the disciples concerning the healing of the lame man, "By what power, or in what name, have ye done this?" (Acts 4:7).

Today the name tells us that God has committed all authority to His Son, so that in the very name itself there is power. But further, we must note in Scripture the recurring expression "*in* the name"—that is to say, the use to which the apostles in fact put that name. It is not only that He *has* such a name, but that we are to *use* it. In three passages in His last discourse the Lord Jesus repeats the words "ask in my name" (see John 14:13–14, 15:16, 16:23–26). He has placed that authority in our hands for us to use. Not only is it His, but it is "given among men" (Acts 4:12). If we do not know our part in it, we suffer great loss.

The power of His name operates in three directions. In our preaching it is effective for the salvation of men (Acts 4:10–12) through the remission of their sins and through their cleansing, justification and sanctification to God (Luke

24:47, Acts 10:43, 1 Cor. 6:11). In our warfare it is mighty against the Satanic powers, to bind and bring them into subjection (Mark 16:17, Luke 10:17–19, Acts 16:18). And as we have already seen, in our asking it is effective toward God, for twice we are told, "Whatsoever ye shall ask . . ."; and twice, "If ye shall ask anything . . ." (John 14:13–14, 15:16, 16:23). Faced with these challenging words, well might we reverently say, "Lord, Your courage is very great!"

For God thus to commit Himself to His servants is indeed a tremendous thing. Glance now with me at three incidents in the Acts which serve to illustrate this further: "Peter said, . . . In the name of Jesus Christ of Nazareth, walk" (Acts 3:6). "Paul . . . turned and said to the spirit, I charge thee in the name of Jesus Christ to come out of her. And it came out that very hour" (Acts 16:18). "Certain . . . exorcists, took upon them to name over them that had the evil spirits the name of the Lord Jesus, saying, I adjure you by Jesus whom Paul preacheth. . . . And the evil spirit answered and said unto them, Jesus I know, and Paul I know, but who are ye?" (Acts 19:13, 15).

Observe first the action of Peter in dealing with the crippled man at the gate. He does not kneel and pray and ask the mind of the Lord first. At once he says, "Walk." He uses the name as if it were his to use, not something far away in heaven. With Paul at Philippi it is the same. He senses in his spirit that the Satanic activity has gone far enough. We are not told that thereupon he pauses to pray. No, his is a true walk before God, and because this is so he can, as a custodian of the name, take action almost as though the power were in himself. He commands, and the evil spirit flees "that very hour."

What is this? It is an example of what I shall call God's

"committal" of Himself to man. God has committed Himself to His servants to act through them as they take action "in the name." And they, what do they do? It is clear that they do nothing of themselves. They use the name. Equally clearly, no other name, whether their own or that of another apostle, will have the same effect. All that takes place results from the impact of the name of the Lord Jesus on the situation, and *they are authorized to use that name.*

God looks at His Son in the glory, not at us here on the earth. It is because He sees us seated with Him *there* that His name and His authority can be entrusted to us here. A simple illustration will help to make this clear.

Some time ago my fellow worker sent to me for a sum of money. I read his letter, prepared what he had asked, and gave the sum to the messenger. Was I right? Yes, certainly. The letter bore my friend's signature, and to me that was sufficient. Should I instead have asked the messenger *his* name and age and employment and native place, and then perhaps sent him away because I objected to what *he* was? No, by no means; for he had come in my friend's name, and I honored that name.

The Divine Self-Committal

It is a mighty thing that God has done in thus committing Himself to His church. In so doing He has entrusted to His servants the greatest possible power; that of One whose dominion is "above . . . every name that is named, not only in this world, but also in that which is to come" (1:21). Jesus is now exalted in heaven, and all His work of saving men, speaking to their hearts and working for them miracles of His grace is done through the medium of His servants as they act *in His name.* Thus, the church's work is His work. The name of Jesus is in fact God's greatest legacy to her, for where such a self-committal of God is really operative, He Himself takes responsibility for what is done in that name. And God *desires* so to commit Himself, for He has allowed Himself no other means for completing His task.

No work is worthy to be called a work of God if God is not, in this sense, committing Himself to it. It is the authorization to use His name that counts. We must be able to stand up and speak *in His name.* If not, our work lacks spiritual impact. But let me tell you, this is not something that can be "worked up" at a time of crisis. It is a fruit of obedience to God and of a resulting spiritual position known and maintained. It is something we must have already if it is to be available in a time of need.

"Jesus I know, and Paul I know." Praise God for the second! The evil powers recognize the Son; the Gospels give us plenty of evidence of this. But there are those also who are in union with the Son, and they too count in Hades. The question is, *Can* God commit Himself thus to you?

Let me illustrate again. If something is to be done in my name, it means that, subject to certain conditions, I give my name to another to use, and that I am then prepared to take responsibility for what he does with it. It may mean, for example, that I give him my checkbook and my signature. Of course, if I am poor, with no personal standing and no bank account, my name is of little moment. I well remember how, as a student, I used to be fond of stamping my name everywhere—on books, papers and anything that came to hand. But when I first had a checkbook and a bank account—

fourteen dollars in the post office—I became very careful over the use of my personal seal for fear someone else should counterfeit it and use it.* My name had become important to me.

How powerful and how wealthy is our Lord Jesus! How precious to Him is His name! If, therefore, He is to take responsibility for everything that happens in consequence, how careful must He be as to how that name is used! I ask you again, *Can* God commit Himself—His "bank balance," His "checkbook," His "signature"—to *you*? That question must be settled first. Then only can you use His name freely. Then only "what things soever ye shall bind on earth shall be bound in heaven" (Matt. 18:18). Then, because of the reality of His committal to you, you can move as a true representative of Him in this world. That is the fruit of union with Him.

Are we in such a union with the Lord that He *will* thus commit Himself to what we are doing? It seems often that we shall be running a big risk in stepping into a situation with only the promises of God to back up our stand. The point is, will God—*can* God—back us up?

Briefly let me outline four essential features of a work to which God can fully commit Himself. The first vital need is of a true revelation to our hearts of the eternal purpose of God. We cannot do without this. If I am working on a building, even as an unskilled laborer, I must know whether

---

* The Chinese custom is for everyone to have his own personal *tu-cheng*, a seal or die bearing the characters of his name carved in wood, stone or ivory in an individual design. The impression is usually made with an opaque red ink. This is felt to be less easily forged than a handwritten signature, and the seal is kept under lock and key and used for signing checks and other personal documents—*Ed.*

the objective is a garage or an airplane hangar or a palace. I must see the plan, or I cannot be an intelligent worker. Today evangelism is assumed by most Christians to be *the* work of God. But evangelism can never be an unrelated thing. It must be integrated with God's whole plan, for it is in fact but a means to an end. That end is the preeminence of the Son of God, and evangelism is bringing in the sons among whom He shall stand preeminent.

In Paul's generation every believer had specific relation to the eternal purpose of God (see especially 4:11–16). That should be no less true of us today. The eyes of God are turning toward His coming kingdom. What we know as organized Christianity will shortly have to make way for something else—the sovereign rule of Christ. But as with the kingdom of Solomon, so now there is first a period of spiritual warfare represented by the reign of David. God is seeking those who will cooperate with Him today in that preparatory warfare.

It is a question of the identification of my purpose with the eternal purpose of God. All Christian work that is not so identified is fragmentary and unrelated, and it does not ultimately get anywhere. We have to seek from God a revelation to our hearts by His Holy Spirit of "the counsel of his will" (see 1:9–12) and then to ask ourselves concerning the work to which we are going back after reading this: "Is it directly related to that?" When that is settled, all the small questions of daily guidance will solve themselves.

Secondly, all work that is going to be effective in the divine purpose must be conceived by God. If we plan work and then ask God to bless it, we need not expect God to commit Himself to it. God's name can never be a "rubber stamp" to authorize work that is ours in conception. True, there may be blessing upon such work, but it will be partial and not full. There can be no "in His name" there; only, alas, our name!

"The Son can do nothing of himself" (John 5:19). How often in the book of Acts we find the Holy Spirit's prohibitions! We read in chapter 16 how Paul and those with him were "forbidden of the Holy Ghost to speak the word in Asia" (16:6). And again, "The Spirit of Jesus suffered them not" (16:7). Yet this book is the book of the *acts* of the Holy Spirit, not of His "inactivities." Too often we think that the actual doing is what matters. We have to learn the lesson of not doing—of keeping quiet for Him. We have to learn that if God does not move, we dare not move. When we have learned this, then it is that He can safely send us forth to speak for Him.

I must have, therefore, a knowledge of God's will in my particular sphere of work. Out of that knowledge only should the work be initiated. The abiding principle of all true Christian work is, "In the beginning God . . ." (Gen. 1:1).

Thirdly, all work, to be effective, must depend for its continuance upon the power of God alone. What is power? We often use the word loosely. We say of a man, "He is a very powerful speaker," but we have to ask ourselves the question: What power is he using? Is it spiritual power, or is it natural power? There is today all too much place given to the power of nature in the service of God. We have got to learn that even where God has initiated a work, if we are trying to accomplish it in our own power, God will never commit Himself to it.

You ask me what I mean by natural power. Put very simply, it is what we can do without the help of God. We give a man the task of organizing something—of planning a gospel campaign or some other Christian activity—because he is naturally a good organizer. But if that is so, how hard will he pray? If he is accustomed to depend on his natural gifts, he may feel no need to cry to God. The trouble with us all is that there are so many things we can do without relying upon God. We must be brought to the place where, naturally gifted though we may be, we dare not speak except in conscious and continual dependence on Him.

Stephen described Moses, after his Egyptian education, as a man "mighty in his words and works" (Acts 7:22). Yet, after God had dealt with him, Moses had to say, "Oh Lord, I am not eloquent, neither heretofore, nor since thou hast spoken unto thy servant; for I am slow of speech, and of a slow tongue" (Exod. 4:10). When a born orator comes to the place of saying, "I can't speak," then he has learned a fundamental lesson and is on the road to real usefulness for God. That discovery involves a crisis and then a lifelong process, both of them implied, surely, in Luke's expression "baptized into the name" (Acts 8:16, 19:5).

That expression points every new believer to the necessity for a fundamental knowledge of the death and resurrection of Christ in its relation to his entire natural man. Somehow, in our history with God, we must experience that initial crippling touch of His hand to weaken our natural strength, so that we stand forth on the ground of resurrection life in Christ alone where death has no longer any claim. After that the circle goes on widening, as fresh areas of our own self-energy are brought under the working of the cross. The way is a costly one, but it is God's sure way to fruitfulness of life and ministry, for it provides Him with the ground He requires in order that He may give His backing to what we do in the name of His Son.

In the work of God today, things are often so constituted that we have no need to rely upon God. But the Lord's verdict upon all such work is uncompromising: "Apart from me ye can do nothing" (John 15:5). Such work as man can do apart from God is wood, hay, stubble—and the test of fire will prove it so. For divine work can only be done with divine power, and that power is to be found in the Lord Jesus alone. It is made available to us in Him on the resurrection side of the cross. That is to say, it is when we have reached the point where in all honesty we cry, "I cannot speak," that we discover God *is* speaking. When we come to an end of our works, His work begins. Thus, the fire in the days to come and the cross today effect the same thing. What cannot stand the cross today will not survive the fire later. If *my* work, which is done in *my* power, is brought to death, how much comes out of the grave? Nothing! Nothing ever survives the cross but what is wholly of God in Christ.

God never asks us to do anything we *can* do. He asks us to live a life which we can never live and to do a work which we can never do. Yet, by His grace, we *are* living it and doing it. The life we live is the life of Christ lived in the power of God, and the work we do is the work of Christ carried on through us by His Spirit whom we obey. Self is the only obstruction to that life and to that work. May we each one pray from our hearts, "O Lord, deal with *me*!"

Finally, the end and object of all work to which God can commit Himself must be His glory. This means that we get nothing out of it for ourselves. It is a divine principle that the less we get of personal gratification out of such a work, the greater is its true value to God. There is no room for glory to man in the work of God. True, there is a deep, precious joy in any service that brings Him pleasure and that opens the door to His working, but the ground of that joy is His glory and not man's. Everything is "to the praise of the glory of his grace" (1:6, 12, 14).

It is when these questions are truly settled between us and God that God will commit Himself—and indeed I believe He will allow us to say then that He *has* to do so. Experience in China has taught us this, that if there is ground for doubt whether our work is of God, then sure enough we find God is reluctant to answer prayer in relation to it. But when it is wholly of Him, He will commit Himself in wonderful ways. Then it is that, in utter obedience to Him, you can use His name, and all hell will have to recognize your authority to do so. When God commits Himself to a thing, then He comes out in power to prove that He is in it and is Himself its Author.

The God of Elijah

Let me give you in closing an experience of my own. A few years after the beginning of our work, we entered upon a period of severe testing. They were days of disappointment and near despair. We had come in for a great deal of criticism and discredit on account of the stand we were taking, resulting in coolness and estrangement, even on the part of the Lord's true people. We had honestly faced and examined the charges made against us, for it is essential always to take criticism seriously and examine it, and not to pass it off with "Oh! He's just *criticizing* me!" Yet we had reason to believe that the Lord was with us, for as a particularly difficult year drew to its close, we were able to reckon that within that period He had given us several hundreds of real conversions.

Then, at the year's end, it seemed that a climax was reached.

Annually for several years it had been our custom at the New Year public holiday to hold a convention in the city for believers of different connections from throughout the province. This year the sponsors of the convention asked me not to attend. The request came as a shock to us. It was, I now realize, an attempt by the Evil One to draw me and my brethren off our ground of rest in Christ. The question was, How would we react?

The New Year holiday is a long one, lasting fully fifteen days; and besides being a suitable period for a convention, it is also the best time for gospel preaching. After seeking the Lord's will, it became clear that He would have us use it for the latter purpose. So I planned to take with me five brothers for a fifteen-day preaching visit to an island off the South China coast. At the last moment another young brother whom I shall call "brother Wu" joined the party. He was only sixteen years of age and had been expelled from school, but he had just lately been born again and there was a marked change in his life. Moreover, he was very eager to come, so after some hesitation I agreed to take him. This made us seven in all.

The island was a fairly large one with a big main village of "six thousand stoves." An old schoolmate of mine was there as headmaster of the village school, and I wrote to him in advance asking for a room in which we might lodge during our stay from January 1 to 15. When, however, we arrived late and in darkness, and when he discovered we had come for gospel preaching, he refused us accommodation. So we sought through the village for somewhere to lodge, until eventually a Chinese herbalist had pity on us and took us in, making us quite comfortable on planks and straw in his attic.

It was not long before the herbalist became our first convert. But though we labored systematically and hard, and though we found the people of the village most courteous, we had very little fruit from the island, and we began to wonder why this was.

On January 9 we were outside preaching. Brother Wu with some others was in one part of the village and suddenly asked publicly, "Why will none of you believe?"

Someone in the crowd replied at once, "We have a god—*one* god—Ta-wang,* and he has never failed us. He is an effective god."

"How do you know that you can trust him?" asked Wu.

"We have held his festival procession every January for 286 years. The chosen day is revealed by divination beforehand, and every year without fail his day is a perfect one without rain or cloud," was the reply.

"When is the procession this year?"

"It is fixed for January 11 at eight in the morning."

"Then," said brother Wu impetuously, "I promise you that it will certainly rain on the eleventh."

At once there was an outburst of cries from the crowd. "That is enough! We don't want to hear any more preaching. If there is rain on the eleventh, then your God is God!"

I was elsewhere in the village when this occurred. As soon as I heard of it, I saw that it was most serious. The news had spread like wildfire, and before long over twenty thousand people would know about it. What were we to do? We stopped

---

*Wang is pronounced with an *a* as in "car" and with the final *ng* very lightly sounded. The name means "Great King."—*Ed.*

our preaching at once and gave ourselves to prayer. We asked the Lord to forgive us if we had overstepped ourselves. I tell you, we were in deadly earnest. What had we done? Had we made a terrible mistake, or dare we ask God for a miracle?

The more you want an answer to prayer from God, the more you desire to be clear with Him. There must be no doubt about fellowship—no shadow between. If your faith were in coincidence, you could afford to have a controversy with Him, but not otherwise. We did not mind being thrown out if we had done something wrong. After all, you can't drag God into a thing against His will! But, we reflected, this would mean an end to the gospel testimony in the island, and Ta-wang would reign supreme forever. What should we do? Should we leave now?

Up to this point we had feared to pray for rain. Then, like a flash, there came the word to me, "Where is the God of Elijah?" It came with such clarity and power that I knew it was from God. Confidently I announced to the brothers, "I have the answer. The Lord will send rain on the eleventh." Together we thanked Him, and then full of praise, we went out—all seven of us—and told everyone. We could accept the devil's challenge in the name of the Lord, and we would broadcast our acceptance.

That evening the herbalist made two very pointed observations. Undoubtedly, he said, Ta-wang *was* an effective god. The devil was with that image. Their faith in him was not groundless. Alternatively, if you preferred a rationalistic explanation, here was a whole village of fishermen. For two or three months on end the men were at sea, and on the fifteenth they would be out again. They, of all people, should know by long experience when it would not rain for two or three days ahead.

This disturbed us. As we went to our evening prayer, we all began once more to pray for rain—*now*! Then it was that there came to us a stern rebuke from the Lord: "Where is the God of Elijah?" Were we going to fight our way through this battle, or were we going to rest in the finished victory of Christ? What had Elisha done when he spoke those words? He had laid claim in his own personal experience to the very miracle that his lord Elijah, now in the glory, had himself performed. In New Testament terms, he had taken his stand by faith on the ground of a finished work.

We confessed our sins again. "Lord," we said, "we don't need rain until the eleventh morning." We went to bed, and next morning (the tenth) we set off for a neighboring island for a day's preaching. The Lord was very gracious, and that day three families turned to Him, confessing Him publicly and burning their idols. We returned late, tired out but rejoicing. We could afford to sleep late tomorrow.

I was awakened by the direct rays of the sun through the single window of our attic. "This isn't rain!" I said. It was already past seven o'clock. I got up, knelt down and prayed. "Lord," I said, "please send the rain!" But once again, ringing in my ears came the word, "Where is the God of Elijah?" Humbled, I walked downstairs before God in silence. We sat down to breakfast—eight of us together, including our host— all very quiet. There was no cloud in the sky, but we knew God was committed. As we bowed to say grace before the food, I said, "I think the time is up. Rain must come now. We can bring it to the Lord's remembrance." Quietly we did so, and this time the answer came with no hint whatever of rebuke in it.

"Where is the God of Elijah?" Even before our "Amen" we heard a few drops on the tiles. There was a steady shower as we ate our rice and were served with a second bowl. "Let us give thanks again," I said, and now we asked God for heavier rain. As we began on that second bowl of rice, the rain was coming down in bucketfuls. By the time we had finished, the street outside was already deep in water, and the three steps at the door of the house were covered.

Soon we heard what had happened in the village. Already, at the first drop of rain, a few of the younger generation had begun to say openly, "There is God; there is no more Ta-wang! He is kept in by the rain." But he wasn't. They carried him out on a sedan chair. Surely he would stop the shower! Then came the downpour. After only some ten or twelve yards, three of the coolies stumbled and fell. Down went the chair and Ta-wang with it, fracturing his jaw and his left arm. Still determined, they carried out emergency repairs and put him back in the chair. Somehow, slipping and stumbling, they dragged or carried him halfway round the village. Then the floods defeated them. Some of the village elders, old men of 60 to 80 years, bareheaded and without umbrellas as their faith in Ta-wang's weather required, had fallen and were in serious difficulties. The procession was stopped, and the idol taken into a house. Divination was made. "Today was the wrong day," came the answer. "The festival is to be on the fourteenth with the procession at six in the evening."

Immediately we heard this there came the assurance in our hearts, "God will send rain on the fourteenth." We went to prayer: "Lord, send rain on the fourteenth at 6:00 P.M. and give us four good days until then." That afternoon the sky cleared, and now we had a good hearing for the gospel. The

Lord gave us over thirty converts—real ones—in the village and in the island during those three short days. The fourteenth broke, another perfect day, and we had good meetings. As the evening approached, we met; and again, at the appointed hour, we quietly brought the matter to the Lord's remembrance. Not a minute late, His answer came with torrential rain and floods as before.

The next day, our time was up, and we had to leave. We have not been back. Other workers asked for those islands, and we never question anyone's claim to a field. But for us the essential point was that Satan's power in that idol had been broken, and that is an eternal thing. Ta-wang was no more "an effective god." The salvation of souls would follow, but was in itself secondary to this vital and unchanging fact.

The impression on us all was a lasting one. God had committed Himself. We had tasted the authority of the name that is above every name—the name that has power in heaven and earth and hell. In those few days we had known what it is to be, as we say, "in the very center of the will of God." Those words were no longer something vague or visionary to us. They described an experience we had ourselves been through. Together we had been granted a brief glimpse of "the mystery of his will" (1:9, 3:9–10). We would go softly all our days. Years later I met "brother Wu." I had lost touch with him, and in the interval he had become an airline pilot. When I asked him whether he still followed the Lord, "Mr. Nee!" he said. "Do you mean to say that after all we went through I could ever forsake Him?"

Do you see what it means to "stand"? We do not try to gain ground; we merely stand on the ground which the Lord Jesus has gained for us, and resolutely refuse to be moved from it. When our eyes are really opened to see Christ as our victorious Lord, then our praise flows forth freely and without restraint. Singing with melody in our hearts to the Lord, we give thanks for all things in His name (5:19–20). Praise that is the outcome of effort has a labored and discordant note, but praise that wells up spontaneously from hearts at rest in Him has always a pure, sweet tone.

The Christian life consists of sitting with Christ, walking by Him and standing in Him. We begin our spiritual life by resting in the finished work of the Lord Jesus. That rest is the source of our strength for a consistent and unfaltering walk in the world. And at the end of a grueling warfare with the hosts of darkness, we are found standing with Him at last in triumphant possession of the field.

"Unto him . . . be the glory . . . for ever" (3:21).

SIT WALK STAND

The Process *of* Christian Maturity

STUDY GUIDE
BY
REBECCA ENGLISH

About This Study Guide

Watchman Nee's little classic, compiled from messages preached in China, touches on important foundational truths—truths easily overlooked in our restless twenty-first century culture. Nee's simple but profound illustrations give a refreshingly clear picture of Scripture's teaching on the Christian life.

Sit, Walk, Stand is a brief discussion of the book of Ephesians. It highlights progressive steps in the life of faith using three words seen repeatedly in Paul's epistle: "sit," "walk" and "stand." In it are helpful insights into biblical doctrine and how that translates to practical Christian living.

At first glance, Nee's straightforward explanations make a study guide seem unnecessary. But in looking deeper, valuable sub-points can be found in each chapter. Careful review of them brings out many details which could be overlooked in initial readings of the book. So believing it will be a helpful addition, CLC Publications has included a study guide in this edition of *Sit, Walk, Stand*.

The guide can be used either individually or in a group setting. Each lesson begins with summary thoughts of the chapter, followed by questions that bring out major themes. Supporting Scripture is also included. Comparing the book's teaching to the Bible will provide a personal grasp of scriptural truth, which is certainly what Nee had in mind.

The guide is broken into four lessons covering the book's introduction and each of the three chapters. The lessons can also be divided into several sessions, since the sections within each lesson can easily lead to extended study. A pad of paper or a journal is recommended for working out questions, especially for individual study or for reflection between group meetings.

As with any theologian's, Nee's conclusions on certain biblical topics may not be fully accepted by every student of Scripture. Regardless of his personal approach, his teaching on the believer's need for continual fullness of the Spirit, for redeeming the time and for knowing the mind of God is certainly scriptural. "If on some point you think differently, that too God will make clear to you" (Phil. 3:15). May you receive much blessing and encouragement from this practical little volume.

Lesson 1

Introduction

Too often in our Christian zeal we set out to please God by whatever practical means are presented to us. It might be through our activity-laden churches, from our own sense of duty or interest, or to meet other people's expectations. The church of today, as in other generations, has largely misunderstood the Christian life to mean action.

But Nee begins with these words: "If the life of a Christian is to be pleasing to God, it must be properly adjusted to Him in all things" (p. 7). He stresses that we have to approach Christian living in a certain order if we are to become mature and useful. Using plain illustrations, he shows that we must be *in* Christ before we can *do* anything for Him.

So what does that mean? To help us see clearly, Nee divides the book of Ephesians into three parts: a doctrinal section (Eph. 1–3) and two practical sections (Eph. 4:1–6:9 and 6:10–24). He then defines these by the keywords "sit," "walk" and "stand."

An Overview

1. To begin, look at the simple outline on page 8. Write it down, and then ponder this statement: "Of all Paul's epistles, it is in Ephesians that we find the highest spiritual truths concerning the Christian life" (p. 8). What are these truths?

2. Spend some time looking over the book of Ephesians to find why it was written, and to whom. Review its subheadings in your Bible and get a feel for its general message.

3. Now look again at Nee's outline. Recognize the natural divisions in the book of Ephesians which form the three sections he suggests. Read specifically verses 2:6, 4:1 and 6:11 to see the source of the three keywords for which *Sit, Walk, Stand* is named.

4. Does the "sit-walk-stand" sequence give you a new perspective on the book of Ephesians and on living the Christian life? In what ways do you think you might be living "out of order" in regard to the progression explained here? How does it affect your usefulness to God?

5. Make a list of things you typically spend time on in any given day. Considering what you actually *do* (not what you *want* to do), what are your priorities? How much do "activities" drive your Christian life?

To be useful in God's hand, a man must be
properly adjusted with respect to all three [aspects]:
his position, his life and his warfare. He falls
short of God's requirements if he underestimates
the importance of any one of them.

Lesson 2

Chapter 1 · Sit

Chapter 1 examines the all-important foundation of the Christian life. Nee looks at three elements of being seated with Christ in order to underscore its significance.

First, he portrays "sitting" as a visual picture of *resting*. Since our human tendency is to act rather than rest, Nee emphasizes that God has a completely different approach to holy living than we do. Thoroughly resting in Christ is vital before we can properly "act" in the Christian life.

Second, Nee explains that it's not just salvation that begins with resting. All growth and service must also come from the foundation of Christ's finished work. So Nee explores *various facets* of the Christian life that must start from a position of rest.

And third, he states that because it is the very nature of God to *give*, our efforts to accomplish our own salvation or growth cause the Lord pain. If we can learn to receive His goodness, we will delight His heart and find true rest in Him.

Section 1
Opening Thoughts

1. Read Ephesians 1–3.

2. "Christianity is a queer business!" proclaims Nee. Living the Christian life is different from what we expect, "for Christianity begins not with a big DO, but with a big DONE." What is Nee driving at here? Consider it in light of Ephesians 1:3 and 2:8 and Hebrews 1:3. What is the fundamental principle on which the Christian life is based "from start to finish" (p. 12)?

3. Ephesians 1:20 and 2:6 assert the facts of Christ's position —and ours with Him. It is not that we are asked to sit down; instead, we're told that in Christ we *are* seated. Luke 14:17 further expresses God's invitation to rest in His finished work. Have you recognized your position of being seated in Christ? Does it seem strange that simply recognizing this could make a difference in the way you feel and act in your Christian life? How could it change your daily living?

4. On pages 13–14 Nee reviews the story of Adam's creation on the sixth day—at the end of God's working. How does this illustrate that our Christian life is to begin from a place of rest? Compare this picture to the New Testament parallel found in John 5:17 and 19:30.

Section 2
"The Range of His Finished Work"

5. Our walk not only begins, but *proceeds*, on the basis of "the finished work of Another" (p. 15). In order to move forward in the Christian life, what is required of us?

6. Ephesians 1:6–7 tells us that our salvation is a gift of God, not gained by works. Further experiences in the Christian life are to develop, in the same way, from our seated position:

   • *The power of the Holy Spirit for service.* According to Acts 2:33, what is the basis for the outpouring of the Holy Spirit? Does the Bible teach us to strive for this blessing (Eph. 1:13; Gal. 3:2, 5)?

   • *Becoming a member of Christ's body.* Ephesians 1:4 affirms God's plan for His people "before the foundation of the world," and Ephesians 4:4 sets forth what the body *is.* Since these facts are already established, how then do we become members of the body (p. 16)?

   • *Our sanctification.* Our holiness, like everything else, proceeds from resting in Christ. What is the picture given in Romans 6:2–4 and Galatians 2:20 to show this?

7. How can we be sure that we are "in Christ" (p. 17, 1 Cor. 1:30, 2 Cor. 1:21)?

8. Romans 6:6 tells us it is a historic fact that we *have been* crucified with Christ. "Do you believe that? It is true! Our crucifixion with Christ is a glorious historic fact. . . . When that fact dawns upon us, and we rest back upon it (Rom 6:11), then we have found the secret of a holy life" (p. 18). Have you ever experienced the relief that comes from recognizing this fact? If so, share or write your testimony. If not, ask the Lord to reveal whatever is holding you back from trusting Him.

9. Nee says that we know "too little of this in experience" (p. 18). Review the illustration he gives about someone making an unkind remark about you. Can you relate? What is the reason for our ongoing difficulty in similar situations?

10. God waits for us to despair of our own efforts to walk before He steps in to help us (pp. 19–20). Why do you think we *want* to keep trying when resting is so much easier? What keeps us insisting on our self-effort?

Section 3
"God the Giver"

11. God delights in giving (Eph. 2:4, 6). When we try to do His work ourselves, we grieve His heart. In the same way, the father of the prodigal son rejoiced in lavishing gifts on his repentant son. Compare the father's response to the returning son (Luke 15:20–24) with his response to the older son's behavior (Luke 15:25–32). He extended love to both, but which son made Him glad?

Write down or discuss personal attitudes in which your life may reflect the older son, and others in which you have experienced the forgiveness and acceptance of the repentant son.

❧

Do you think that if you cease trying to please
God, your good behavior will cease? If you leave all the
giving and all the working to God, do you think
the result will be less satisfactory than if you do some
of it? It is when we seek to do it ourselves that we place
ourselves back again under the Law.

Lesson 3

Chapter 2 · Walk

In chapter 2 Nee unfolds the teaching of Ephesians regarding practical Christian living. This chapter too is divided into three general sub-thoughts on the matter.

Nee begins by restating that our conduct ("walking") never develops correctly unless we are first at rest ("sitting"). However, once we understand the doctrinal truth of our rest in Christ, the *practical* outworking of the Christian life will follow. This becomes especially visible in the area of relationships with others.

He then impresses on us the *standard* of walking to which we are called. It is the perfect, impossible standard of the love of God! Human effort tries to set its own measure of right and wrong, but again we are brought to the fact that it is only Christ's life in us that is sufficient for this demand.

Nee's third focus in walking concerns *timing*. Since the word "walk" denotes progress—moving toward a goal—Nee challenges us to redeem the time by being continually filled with the Holy Spirit. We can waste time and still be saved "as through fire" (1 Cor. 3:15), but we will have lost much through the foolish squandering of our lives.

Section 1
Opening Thoughts

1. Read Ephesians 4:1–6:9.

2. It has now been well established that "all true spiritual experience begins from rest." But it's also true that "it does not end there" (p. 23). If "sitting" describes our doctrinal position in Christ, what does "walking" represent (p. 24)? Write down the definitions of the word "walk" that Nee gives.

3. A principal element of our Christian "walk" concerns our relationships. In reality, the way we relate to others exposes the true state of our inner "sitting" with Christ (pp. 24–25). Look at Ephesians 4:25–32 and consider whether your life exhibits the "new man" described there. If not, what can you do about it?

Section 2
"The Perfection of the Father"

4. God's standard is perfection (Matt. 5:48) as conveyed in the Sermon on the Mount (Matt. 5–7). This is an impossible demand! Based on principles from lesson 2, what is God's provision for us in approaching such a standard?

5. Nee states, "Nothing has done greater damage to our Christian testimony than our trying to be right and demanding right of others. . . . As Christians our standard of living can never be 'right or wrong,' but the cross" (p. 27). What is this "principle of the cross" that Nee refers to (also see p. 35)? Where do our standards of "right and wrong" come from? What does it mean to do "more than what is right" (p. 28)?

6. Knowing we cannot attain holiness through our efforts to be "right," Nee asks, "What is the secret strength of the Christian life? From where does it derive its power?" (p. 29). What answer does he give? What do Ephesians 3:20 and Colossians 1:29 tell us?

7. God has provided a way for us to attain His perfection, but we must be *willing* for God to work in us so we can "work out our own salvation" (Phil. 2:12–13). "Until we are willing for God to work it in, it is useless for us to try to work it out" (p. 30). Take a few minutes to reflect on attitudes in your life that may manifest unwillingness to give Christ lordship of your spiritual life.

8. Too many Christians are acting, says Nee. This is the result of self-effort and, once more, reveals our desire to be "right." Think about these two quotes: "The all-important rule is not to 'try' but to 'trust'" (p. 33) and "Our life *is* the life of Christ, mediated in us by the indwelling Holy Spirit Himself, and the law of that life *is* spontaneous" (pp. 33–34). How would these truths address our problem of "acting"?

9. If our *doctrine* (Eph. 1–3) is not followed by real Christian *living* (Eph. 4–6), then we are a contradiction. Nee says that it would be better to have no doctrine than to be a contradiction (p. 35). Does Scripture support such a statement (compare to James 2:14–26)? Can you find other passages that shed light on how Christian behavior should follow correct doctrine?

Section 3
"Redeeming the Time"

10. Besides speaking of our conduct, the word "walk" speaks also of progress, of moving toward a goal. How does this progressive aspect of walking apply to Scripture's exhortation to redeem the time (p. 36, Eph. 5:15–17)?

11. God is looking for firstfruits (Rev. 14:1–5). Firstfruits, according to Nee, are not necessarily of better quality, but represent those saints who wisely redeemed the time and were wholly dedicated to the Lord. Their lives were more fully used to God's glory, and as such they become a special offering to Him (pp. 37–38). Are you redeeming the time—living fully for the glory of God? List or discuss practices in your life that may, or may not, result in eternal value.

12. Nee uses the parable of the wise and foolish virgins (Matt. 25:1–13) to illustrate our need to be *continually* filled with the Holy Spirit (Eph. 5:18). Continual filling will make us fruitful in service, prepare us for the return

of Christ (Matt. 25:13) and result in oneness among believers (Eph. 4:3, 15–16, 5:19; Rev. 14:3). What are some practical ways that we as Christians can redeem the time? What are some things that, although good, can waste our time in light of eternity?

13. Like Paul, we should press forward eagerly (1 Cor. 9:23–27, Phil. 3:8–14) because the days are evil (Eph. 5:16). What are some evidences in our culture that "the days are evil"? Although political activism and other such practices can be useful in opposing wicked plans, what does Scripture indicate is God's will for believers living in evil days?

❧

God has given us Christ. There is nothing now
for us to receive outside of Him. The Holy Spirit has
been sent to produce what is of Christ in us; not
to produce anything that is apart from or outside of
Him. . . . What we show forth outwardly is
what God has first put within.

Lesson 4

Chapter 3 · Stand

This final chapter on "standing" focuses on the important principle of spiritual warfare. Nee breaks his teaching into the customary three sections; he then concludes with a story from which we can gain some extra insight.

The chapter begins with a general explanation of spiritual "standing" as it pertains to our personal lives. Standing depicts a defensive posture in our warfare in which we *hold fast* the ground that Christ has already won. Nee reiterates that if we are not first seated, then walking from that position of rest, we will not be able to effectively stand against the Enemy.

The next concept is more in-depth. Though our warfare is mainly from a defensive standpoint, there is also a sense in which we are to take the offense. This is when we must lay hold of God's promises by faith, through prayer and/or action. This can be a difficult subject to understand and is interpreted by Christians in various ways. Nee is basically saying that offensive warfare can only effectively be done *in Jesus' name*—when it is backed and approved by God Himself, and not just something we hope He will approve.

Third, Nee looks further at using the name of Jesus as it regards service to Him. He marvels at the boldness of God in entrusting His name to us. He then outlines four characteristics of the kind of ministry to which God will fully commit Himself.

Nee finishes with a personal testimony to bring home the outworking of these principles. It is stirring to see how God did commit Himself to work that was done in His name as Nee and his co-workers sought to know His mind in the matter at hand.

Section 1
Opening Thoughts

1. Read Ephesians 6:10–24.

2. Christians must be prepared for conflict. But if we have not first learned to "sit" and then to "walk," we will not be able to effectively "stand." Nee warns, "If [any Christian] is deficient in either of these [sitting or walking], he will find that all the talk about spiritual warfare remains only talk; he will never know its reality. Satan can afford to ignore him, for he does not count for anything" (p. 46). Have you encountered this reality in your life or ministry? Talk about or write down some examples.

3. We have already learned that both sitting and walking proceed from Christ's power in us (Eph. 1:19 and 3:16). Compare these two verses to Ephesians 6:10 to see the continued necessity of resting in Christ in this matter of spiritual warfare.

4. Look more closely at Ephesians 6:10–17. The weapons
    show us that our warfare is, in the main, defensive. Thus,
    we are called to stand on the ground Christ already gained.
    Nee says that "when you fight to *get* the victory, then you
    have lost the battle at the very outset" (p. 49). Why is this
    so?

5. "Satan's primary object is not to get us to sin, but simply to
    make it easy for us to do so by getting us off the ground of
    perfect triumph onto which the Lord has brought us" (p.
    49). What does it mean to get "off the ground of perfect
    triumph"? Refer to Romans 8:33–37 for insight into this.

Section 2
"In His Name"

6. Though our warfare is largely defensive, there is one sense
    in which it is offensive. Though Christ has already won
    (Eph. 1:21–22), we do not yet see everything subject to
    Him (Heb. 2:8)—and for now the Enemy is occupying
    territory that is rightly God's. Here is where we use our one
    weapon of offense, the sword of the Spirit. Read Ephesians
    6:17–18. What does offensive warfare consist of?

7. Nee highlights two passages on prayer which focus on the
    use of Jesus' name (p. 52). Read these two passages (Matt.
    18:18–20; John 16:23–24, 26) and then read the para-
    graph on page 52 that begins with the words, "None can
    be saved . . ." What does it mean for us to use the name of
    Jesus?

8. The power of His name operates in three directions (pp. 53–54):

   • for *salvation* (Acts 40:10–12) and the ensuing process of *sanctification* (Luke 24:47, Acts 10:43, 1 Cor. 6:11)

   • for *spiritual warfare* in binding the Enemy (Mark 16: 17, Luke 10:17–19, Acts 16:18)

   • for *asking* of God (John 14:13–14, 15:16, 16:23)

   Read the above referenced verses for examples of using the power of Jesus' name. What are some personal experiences in which you have seen the Lord's name used in any of these directions?

Section 3
"The Divine Self-Committal"

9. Praying and acting "in the name of Jesus" results from doing those things to which He has committed Himself —things to which He can "sign His name." When God commits Himself to us on an issue, we can act with authority (Eph. 1:21, Matt. 18:18).

10. Ministry done in the name of Jesus will have the following characteristics:

    • *It will be born from a revelation of God's eternal purpose through it.* What is God's ultimate goal in our service to Him (p. 58)? How can we know the personal role

God wants us to play in it (Eph. 4:11–16, 1:9–12)? What is the purpose of organized Christianity?

- *It will be a work that is conceived by God.* Why is it that we tend to plan our work and then ask God to bless it? What kind of fruit comes of service done in this way (pp. 58–59)? How did Jesus and Paul carry out their ministries in light of this truth (John 5:19, Acts 16:6–7)?

- *It will continue in dependence upon God alone for its empowering and enabling.* The church has become accustomed to leaning on natural ability or common sense in assigning ministry. But work done in this way does not require the power of God. What does John 15:5 say about our ability to bear fruit? Therefore, what kind of fruit comes from ministry that is run purely on practical lines, and what will happen to it (1 Cor. 3:12–15)?

- *It is to the end that God is glorified.* What are we to get out of our service to God? What is the difference between what we will receive and what God should receive (pp. 61–62, Eph. 1:6, 12, 14)?

A Testimony
"The God of Elijah"

11. In following the will of God, we will face criticism. We must know His will in order to be certain of working in

His name. Read John 7:17, Romans 12:2 and Ephesians 1:8–10. Can we be certain of knowing God's will in our own lives? How can we discern His voice?

12. How did Nee know for certain that the words "Where is the God of Elijah?" (2 Kings 2:1–14) were God's message for him? Was this faith or presumption? Can we know (Eph. 1:9, 3:10)?

꿏

The Christian life consists of sitting with Christ, walking by Him and standing in Him. We begin our spiritual life by resting in the finished work of the Lord Jesus. That rest is the source of our strength for a consistent and unfaltering walk in the world. And at the end of a grueling warfare with the hosts of darkness, we are found standing with Him at last in triumphant possession of the field.

"Unto him . . . be the glory . . . for ever."